HOW TO CURL PLASTIC LACING (Adult supervision is required when kids

flat lacing
curling rod (pencil, dowel, skewer, knitting needle, etc.) as specified for
electric skillet (or 9"x13" pan) of boiling water
9"x13" pan of ice water
spring clothespins, tongs, towel

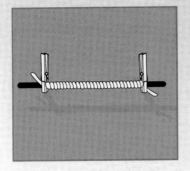

1 Use a clothespin to fasten one end of the lacing to the curling rod. Wind it tightly around the rod and clothespin the other end.

2 Place the wrapped rod in a pan of boiling water. Slowly count to 30.

3 Use tongs to remove the rod from the water and place it in ice water. Slowly count to 30.

4 Remove and towel dry. Remove the clothespins, carefully loosen the lacing from the rod and slide it off.

BLACK & PINK CURLS SET

5 yards of black flat plastic lacing
2¹/₂ yards of pink round plastic lacing
ten ¹/₄" wide pink pony beads
four ¹/₂" wide turquoise/black carved plastic
*   beads*
two silver ear wires
needle nose pliers
three 11" bamboo skewers with pointed ends
*   removed (for curling rods)*
curling supplies (see above)
basic supplies (see page 1)

1 Wrap black lacing around the skewers and curl (see above). Cut the curled lengths into seven 3" long curls.

2 **Each earring:** Hold two curls together and fold in half. Push the folded ends through a pink bead, turquoise bead and pink bead. Pull them out ¹/₄" to form a loop. Use needle nose pliers to attach the ear wire to the earring loop. Repeat for the second earring.

3 **Choker:** Cut a 1¹/₂-yard length of pink lacing. Fold in half and tie an overhand knot (see page 18) ¹/₂" from the fold, forming a loop. Hold the loose ends together and thread on a curl, pink bead, turquoise bead, pink bead and black curl. Tie an overhand knot 2" from the end, place a pink bead on both strands, then knot again. Trim the ends.
To clasp: Slip the end bead through the beginning loop.

4 **Bracelet:** Follow step 3 but use a 1-yard length of pink lacing and cut the remaining curl in half.

2

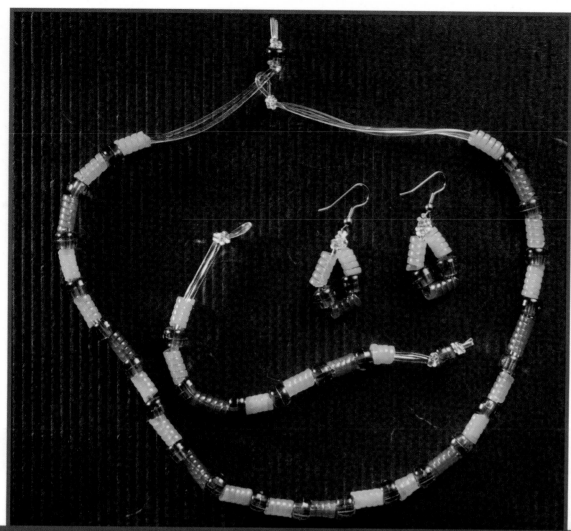

transparent flat plastic lacing, 2 yards each: blue, green, yellow

3¹/₃ yards of clear round plastic lacing

thirty-three ¹/₄" wide transparent brown pony beads

2 gold ear wires

needle nose pliers

three 11" bamboo skewers with pointed ends removed (for curling rods)

curling supplies (see page 2)

basic supplies (see page 1)

SPRINGS & BEADS

1 Wrap each 2-yard flat lacing length around a skewer. Follow the curling instructions on page 2. Cut the curled lengths into 13 yellow, 11 green and 11 blue ¹/₃"-¹/₂" long pieces for springs.

2 **Each earring:** Cut a 12" length of clear lacing. String a spring of each color and a bead on one 12" length. Repeat, alternating colors for a total of three springs and two beads. Hold the ends together, forming a loop, and tie an overhand knot (see page 18) close to the springs; trim the ends close to the knot. Use needle nose pliers to attach the ear wire to one strand of the knot. Repeat for the other earring.

3 **Necklace:** Cut a 1¹/₂-yard length of clear lacing. Fold in half and tie an overhand knot to form a ¹/₂" loop. String a spring and bead over both strands referring to the large photo for color placement. Repeat, alternating colors for a total of 22 springs and 21 beads. Tie an overhand knot 2" from the end, slide on a bead, then tie another overhand knot. **To clasp:** slip the end bead through the beginning loop.

4 **Bracelet:** Follow step 3 but use a 1-yard length of clear lacing, seven springs and six beads.

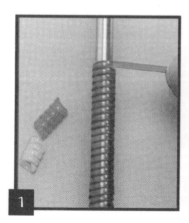

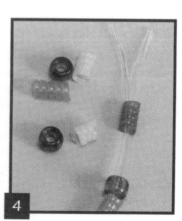

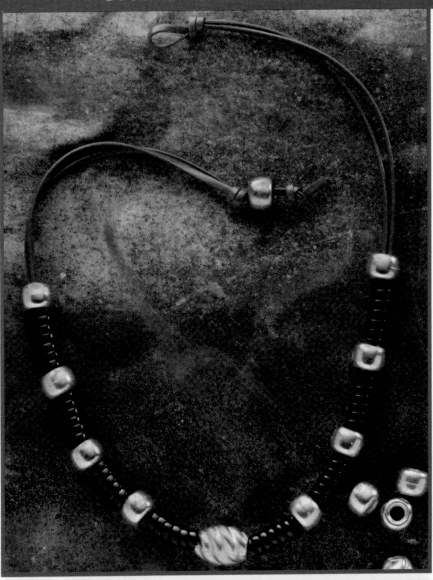

flat plastic lacing: 1½ yards of black, 1½ yards of matte brown
nine ¼" wide copper pony beads
½" long copper bead with lengthwise hole
11" long bamboo skewer with pointed ends removed (curling rod)
curling supplies (see page 2)
basic supplies (see page 1)

1 Wrap the black lacing around the skewer. Follow the curling instructions on page 2. Cut the curled lengths into eight ½" curls for springs.

2 Fold the brown lacing length in half. Tie an overhand knot (see page 18) ½" below the fold to form a loop. Place a pony bead and spring over both strands. Repeat for a total of four beads and four springs. Slide the large copper bead over all the strands, then repeat the four beads and springs pattern starting with a spring. Tie an overhand knot 2" from the end, slide on a pony bead, then knot again. **To clasp:** slip the end bead through the beginning loop.

24" length of black flat plastic lacing
48" length of clear/silver glitter flat lacing
⅜" wide silver melon bead
basic supplies (see page 1)

1 Fold the black lacing in half and place the end of the clear/glitter length in the fold. Tie all three lengths in an overhand knot (see page 18) ½" from the fold to form a loop.

2 Use the clear/glitter lacing to zipper braid for 3". Slide the melon bead over all the lacing lengths. Zipper braid for 3".

3 Tie the ends in an overhand knot. **To clasp:** Tie the ends through the beginning loop.

HOW TO WRAP A BRACELET BLANK

plastic lacing, aluminum bracelet blank, transparent tape (we used white for illustration purposes)

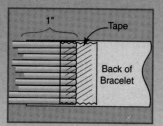

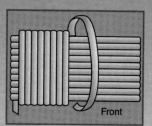

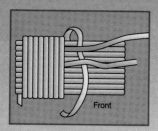

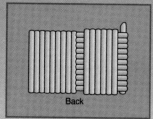

1 Tape the lengthwise strands to the back of the bracelet blank, then bring them around to the front. Smooth them down and hold them in place.

2 At the back, slide the end of the wrapping strand under the taped strands. Begin wrapping. Be careful to keep the lengthwise strands flat and don't let the wrapping strand twist.

3 To make the designs, lift horizontal strands and wrap the vertical strand under them as instructed in the project.

4 When you are ½"-¾" from the end of the bracelet, fold the lengthwise strands to the back. Continue wrapping to the end of the bracelet. Cut the vertical strand at an angle, leaving a 3" tail. Run the angled end under the lengthwise strands, pull all the ends tight and trim excess. Bend the bracelet to fit your wrist.

THUNDERBIRD KEY RING

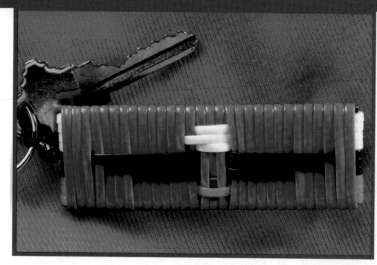

flat plastic lacing: ²/₃ yard white, ²/₃ yard brown,
   ½ yard tangerine, 2½ yards blue
1"x6" aluminum bracelet blank
1" wide silver split ring
tin snips or utility scissors (to cut metal)
wrapping supplies (see above)
basic supplies (see page 1)

1 Cut a 1"x6" bracelet blank in half crosswise to make one that measures 1"x3". Save one piece for another project. Cut four white lengths, three tangerine lengths and two brown lengths, each 5" long. Cut a 12" brown length. Fold it in half through the split ring and tie in an overhand knot (see page 18). Trim one end to ¾".

2 Tape the cut strands lengthwise to the blank (see wrapping instructions above) in this order: white, brown, tangerine. Slip the blue strand end under the lengthwise strand ends as shown in step 2 of the wrapping instructions.

3 Follow the diagram on page 6 and the picture below to make the design, lifting the lengthwise strands and placing the blue strand under them.

4 Glue the lengthwise strands to the back of the blank before you make your final 2-3 wraps. Follow step 4 of the wrapping instructions.

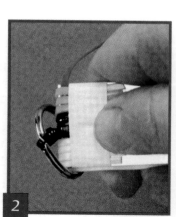

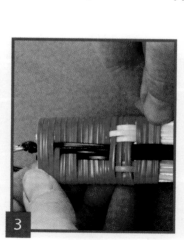

flat plastic lacing: 1¹/₂
  yards of white, 2¹/₂
  yards of bright pink
¹/₂" wide white heart
  pony bead
1"x6" aluminum
  bracelet blank
1" wide silver split ring
tin snips or utility scissors (to cut metal)
wrapping supplies (see
  page 5)
basic supplies (see
  page 1)

I LOVE YOU KEY RING

1 Cut a 1"x6" bracelet blank in half crosswise to make one that measures 1"x3". Save one for another project. Cut eight 5" and one 12" white lacing lengths. Fold the 12" length in half through the split ring and tie in an overhand knot (see page 18). Trim one end to ³/₄".

2 Follow the wrapping instructions on page 5 to tape the white strands lengthwise to the blank (we used white tape for illustration purposes). Make sure the strand attached to the ring is in the center as shown. Slide the end of the pink lacing strand under the taped down strands at the back of the blank.

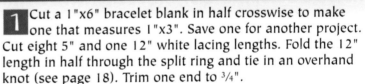

3 Make the design by lifting the white strands and wrapping the pink strand under them as shown in the diagram and the photo below. Add the bead on the sixth wrap after completing the I.

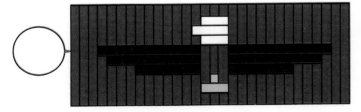

4 **To finish:** Follow step 4 of the wrapping instructions. Glue the lengthwise strands to the back of the blank before you make your final 2-3 wraps.

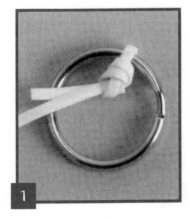

1

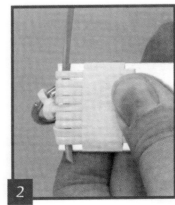

2

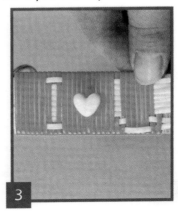

3

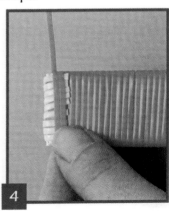

4

BROWN & BLACK BRACELET AND CHRISTMAS TREE BRACELET

for each:
1"x6" aluminum bracelet blank
wrapping supplies (see page 5)
basic supplies (see page 1)

black and brown bracelet:
flat plastic lacing: 2½ yards of matte black, 5 yards of matte brown

Christmas tree bracelet:
flat plastic lacing: 2½ yards of green translucent, 5 yards of white
dimensional paint: gold glitter, red

1 **Christmas tree bracelet:** Cut eleven 8" green lengths. Follow the wrapping instructions on page 5 to tape the strands lengthwise to the bracelet.

2 Following the wrapping instructions, wrap the white lacing five times. Lift the bottom two green strands and wrap the white lacing under them once. Next, lift the bottom four black strands and wrap under them.

3 Continue wrapping and lifting to complete five green triangles. Follow the wrapping instructions on page 5 to finish, but don't bend it to fit your arm.

4 Use gold paint to make a dot at the top of each tree. Use red paint to make dots randomly on the trees for ornaments. Let dry; bend to fit your arm. **Brown and black bracelet:** Follow steps 1-3, using the brown lacing for the lengthwise strands. Bend to fit your arm.

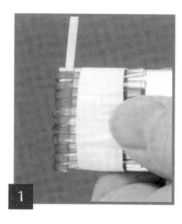

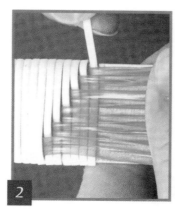

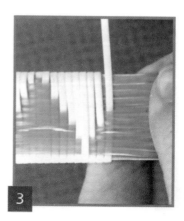

NECKERCHIEF SLIDE

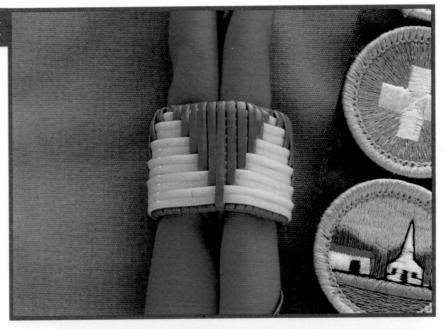

flat plastic lacing: 1²/₃ yards of yellow, 2¹/₂ yards of blue
1"x6" aluminum bracelet blank
tin snips or utility scissors (to cut metal)
wrapping supplies (see page 5)
basic supplies (see page 1)

1 Cut a 1"x6" bracelet blank in half cross-wise to make one that measures 1"x3". Save one for another project. Cut eleven 5" yellow lengths. Follow the basic wrapping instructions on page 5 and the triangle diagram on page 7 to complete two yellow triangles. Finish as directed on page 5, bending the finished blank into a ring to hold a neckerchief.

PEACE SIGN PENDANT

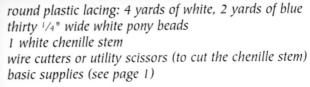

round plastic lacing: 4 yards of white, 2 yards of blue
thirty ¹/₄" wide white pony beads
1 white chenille stem
wire cutters or utility scissors (to cut the chenille stem)
basic supplies (see page 1)

1 Slide 20 beads onto the chenille stem. Slide the stem ends into the last beads to form a circle. If the stem is not completely covered by the beads, use wire cutters to cut the ends off.

2 Cut the white lacing length in half. Fold one in half over the beaded circle. Hold the ends together and slide on three beads. Place the other 2-yard length between the folded strands crosswise across the circle. Slide two beads onto each side. Wrap the loose ends around the circle as shown, then back through the two beads.

3 Bring all four lacing ends through the last three beads. At the top of the circle, separate the strands so there are two strands on each side of circle. Tie all the strands in an overhand knot (see page 18).

4 Divide the white strands into two groups with two strands each. Fold the blue length in half, then place the fold at the knot. Braid both groups (see page 12). **To clasp:** Tie the braids together in a tight over-hand knot.

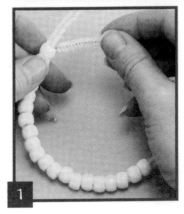

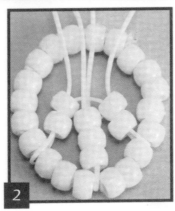

8

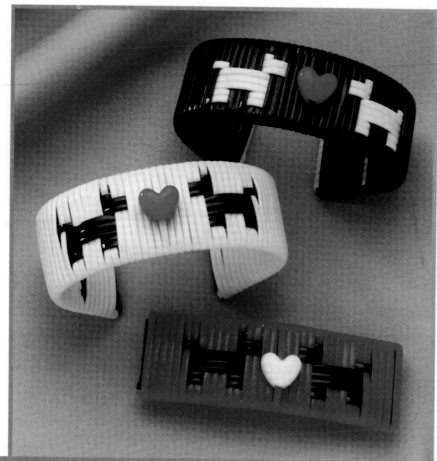

for each:
wrapping supplies (see page 5)
basic supplies (see page 1)

black bracelet:
1"x6" aluminum bracelet blank
flat plastic lacing: 2⅓ yards of white, 5 yards of black
½" wide red heart pony bead with lengthwise hole

white bracelet:
1"x6" aluminum bracelet blank
flat plastic lacing: 2⅓ yards of black, 5 yards of white
½" wide red heart pony bead with lengthwise hole

barrette:
1"x6" aluminum bracelet blank
flat plastic lacing: 1½ yards of black, 2⅓ yards of red
½" wide white heart pony bead with lengthwise hole
2½" barrette back
tin snips or utility scissors (to cut metal)

SCOTTIES & HEARTS WRAPPED SET

1 **White bracelet:** Cut ten 8" black lacing lengths. Tape them lengthwise to the back of the blank as shown in the wrapping instructions on page 5. Follow steps 2 and 3 of the wrapping instructions to wrap the white lacing around the blank and begin making the design (see diagram).

2 After finishing the first Scottie, wrap four times over all the horizontal strands. Slip a red heart bead onto the white strand and slide it up to the center. Wrap four times, then start the other Scottie. Finish wrapping the bracelet, then tuck the end in as shown in step 4 of the wrapping instructions. **Black bracelet:** Repeat steps 1-2 using white lacing for the lengthwise strands and black for the wrapping strand.

3 **Barrette:** Cut a bracelet blank in half crosswise to 1"x3". Save one piece for another project. Cut ten 5" black lacing lengths. Tape them lengthwise to the blank back. Wrap red lacing around the blank and make one Scottie. Wrap two times, then slip a white heart bead onto the red strand. Slide it up to the center, then wrap two more times. Make another Scottie. Finish wrapping the blank, then tuck in the end.

4 Bend the wrapped blank so it matches the curve of the barrette. Glue the barrette to the back.

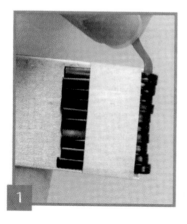

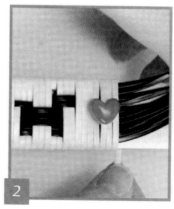

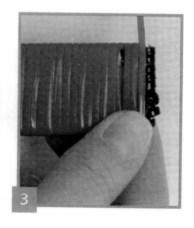

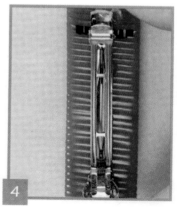

HOW TO SQUARE KNOT BRAID (COBRA BRAID)

4 lengths of plastic lacing as specified for the project, with 2 twice as long as the others

1 Knot all four strands together. Label the strands A, B, C, and D—A and D are the long strands.

2 Place strand A **over** B and C and **under** D. Bring strand D behind C and B, up and through the loop of A from back to front. Pull the working strands (A and D) tightly around the core strands (B and C) each time you complete a knot.

3 Place strand D **behind** B and C and **over** A. Bring strand A over the core strands and through the loop of D from front to back. Tighten as before.

4 Continue braiding, repeating steps 2 and 3, to the desired length. Knot the ends together.

RAINBOW CHOKER & KEY RING SET

flat plastic lacing: 8¹/₃ yards of matte black
¹/₄" wide pony beads: 2 each of red, orange, yellow, green, blue, purple
1" wide silver split ring
basic supplies (see page 1)

1 **Choker:** Cut a 1-yard and a 5-yard black lacing length. Fold the 1-yard length in half. Tie the center of the 5-yard length around it in a square knot (see above) ¹/₄" below the fold.

2 Follow step 1 of the square knot braid instructions above to arrange and label the strands. Make a 4¹/₂" square knot braid. Slide a red bead over the two center strands. Tie a square knot. Repeat for all the beads, placing them on the strands in rainbow order as shown in the large photo.

3 Make another 4¹/₂" square knot braid. Tie in an overhand knot (see page 18). **To clasp:** Tie the end strands through the beginning loop.

4 **Key ring:** Cut a 24" length and a 1¹/₂ yard length of black lacing. Fold the 24" length in half through the ring. Tie the 1¹/₂-yard length in a square knot below the ring. Square knot braid for ¹/₂". Slide the red bead on the center strands, then tie a square knot. Repeat for all the beads, placing them in rainbow order. Tie the ends in an overhand knot. Trim the ends to 2".

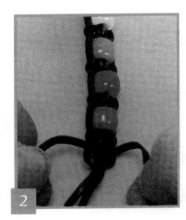

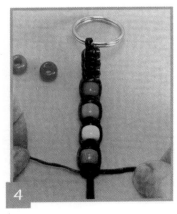

each:
two 5mm wide wiggle eyes
basic supplies (see page 1)

snail:
2 yards of bright green flat plastic lacing
green chenille stem
1" wide bright green pom pom
mini spring clothespin, pencil
1¹⁄₂"x¹⁄₂" self-adhesive magnet

dragonfly:
1¹⁄₂ yards of tangerine flat plastic lacing
2 orange chenille stems
¹⁄₂" wide pom poms: 1 orange, 1 yellow
³⁄₄" wide orange pom pom
mini spring clothespin
1¹⁄₂"x¹⁄₂" self-adhesive magnet

caterpillar:
2 yards of turquoise flat plastic lacing
royal blue chenille stem
³⁄₄" wide royal blue pom pom
pencil

CRAZY CRITTER CLIPS

1 **Caterpillar and snail:** Fold the chenille stem in half, then place the lacing center in the fold. Tie the lacing in a square knot braid (see page 10) around the entire stem. Knot and trim the ends. Save the leftover lacing pieces for step 3. **Dragonfly:** Repeat, but braid for only 2¹⁄₂".

2 **Caterpillar:** Glue the pom pom to the top of the braid end as shown in the large photo. **Snail:** Curl the braid around a pencil as shown, then glue the 1" pom pom to top of the braid end. **Dragonfly:** Cut a chenille stem to 8" long and glue the ends together to form a loop. Pinch the center and twist twice to make the wings. Glue the pom poms to the braid as shown in the large photo.

3 **For each face:** Glue two eyes to the large pom pom front. Tie one end of a leftover plastic lacing piece from step 1 in an overhand knot (see page 18) and trim close to the knot. Cut the entire piece to 1" long. Repeat, then glue them to the top of the head for antennae.

4 **Snail and dragonfly:** Glue the bottom of each body to a clothespin, then stick a magnet to the other side of the clothespin. **Caterpillar:** Wrap the caterpillar around a pencil as shown, use it as a bookmark or fold it accordion-style and glue it to a clothespin.

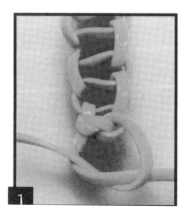

HOW TO BRAID
3 lengths of plastic lacing as specified for the project

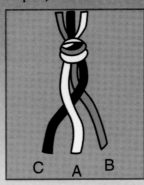

1 Knot all three strands together. Label the strands A, B and C.

2 Bring C over B and A over C.

3 Bring B over A. Tighten and repeat to the desired length.

DAISY CHAIN LANYARD

round plastic lacing: 3 yards of white, 1 yard of bright green
1/4" wide pony beads: 18 white, 9 bright green, 3 yellow
1" long silver lanyard hook
2 1/2" long silver whistle
basic supplies (see page 1)

1 Slide the lanyard hook to the center of the white lacing and tie an overhand knot (see page 18).

2 To make a daisy, slip two white beads onto a lacing end. Place the end of the other strand through the beads from the opposite direction as shown. Pull until the beads are centered over the knot. Repeat with a white, a yellow and a white bead, then repeat with two white beads. Slide three green beads over both strands. Repeat the daisy and green beads pattern twice.

3 Slip the end of the green lacing through the last three green beads and tie it in an overhand knot. Place the beaded end in a split ring or have someone hold it and braid the three strands together (see braiding instructions above). Tie an overhand knot 3"-4" from the ends. Attach the whistle to the hook.
To clasp: Tie the ends through the braid.

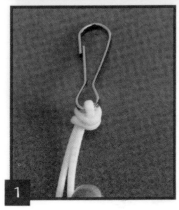

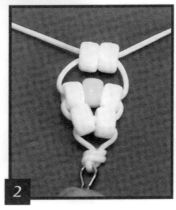

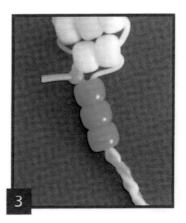

for each:
basic supplies (see page 1)
tracing paper
transfer paper
pencil

skier:
flat plastic lacing: 1½ yards of red, 2½ yards of
    turquoise
chenille stems: 1 red, 1 blue, 1 white
25mm wide wooden bead with pre-painted face
    and ¼" hole
three ¼" wide bright green pony beads
½" wide pom poms: 4 black, 2 green
¼" wide red pom pom
pieces of gold felt: ¼"x6", 4"x2½"
two ¼" wide clear buttons with holes
2 wooden craft sticks

skater:
flat plastic lacing: 1½ yards of orange, 2 yards of
    bright green, ½ yard of turquoise
chenille stems: 1 orange, 1 green
25mm wide wooden bead with pre-painted face
    and ¼" hole
three ¼" wide blue pony beads
½" wide pom poms: 4 white, 2 blue
¼" wide orange pom pom
pieces of green felt: ¼"x6", 4"x2½"
2 silver paper clips

WINTER BENDERS

1 **Skier:** To make arms, cut the red chenille stem to 8". Fold the stem in half and center the red lacing length crosswise through the fold. Square knot braid (see page 10) the strands around the stem. Tie the ends in a knot, then trim. Repeat with the entire blue chenille stem and turquoise lacing to make the legs.

2 Fold an 18" length of turquoise lacing in half over the center of the legs. Slide three green beads over both strands. Wrap the turquoise lacing over the center of the arms and slide on the face bead. Tie an overhand knot (see page 18) at the top of the head to hold all the body parts together. Do not trim the ends.

3 Transfer the hat and scarf patterns on page 18 to gold felt; cut out. Glue the hat into a cone shape, leaving the point open. Slip the hat over the lacing at the top of the head and slide it down; glue. Knot the hanger

½" from the end. Glue the ¼" pom pom to hat point. Knot the scarf around the neck; glue. Glue the green pom poms to the arm ends for mittens. Glue two black pom poms together, then glue them to the end of the leg for a boot. Repeat with the remaining black pom poms.

4 Cut the white chenille stem into two 4" lengths for ski poles. Glue a pole to each mitten. Slip a button onto each pole; glue. Glue craft sticks to the bottom of the boots for skies.

5 **Skater:** Repeat steps 1-3 using the orange chenille stem and lacing for the arms, the green chenille stem and lacing for the legs and turquoise lacing to hold the body parts together. Glue a paper clip to the bottom of each boot for a skate.

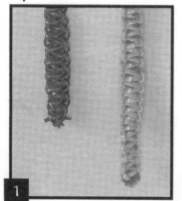

HOW TO HALF KNOT BRAID

3-4 lengths of plastic lacing as specified for the project, with 2 twice as long as the others

1 Knot all three strands together. Label the strands A, B and C,—A and C are the long strands.

2 Place A over B and behind C. Wrap C behind B and through the loop made by A.

3 Wrap C over B and behind A. Place A behind B and through the loop made by C.

NEON PENDANT & BRACELET

6¹/₂ yards of neon green round plastic lacing
¹/₄" wide neon pony beads: 6 orange, 6 green, 6 yellow, 6 pink
yellow chenille stem
wire cutters or utility scissors (to cut the chenille stem)
basic supplies (see page 1)

1 **Bracelet:** Cut the green lacing into an 18" and a 2-yard length. Fold the 2-yard length in half and place the 18" length end in the fold. Tie both pieces in an overhand knot (see page 18) ¹/₂" from the fold to form a loop. Half knot braid (see instructions above) for 3". Slide four beads over all the lacing strands. Half knot braid for 3". Tie the ends in an overhand knot. **To clasp:** Slip the end knot through the beginning loop.

2 **Pendant:** Fold the remaining lacing in half. Tie the ends in an overhand knot (see page 18). Place the fold in a split ring or ask someone to hold it. Twist the knotted end very tightly.

3 Remove the split ring and fold the twisted length in half. The two sets of twists should twist together. Tie the ends in an overhand knot.

4 Slide 20 beads onto the chenille stem following the large photo for color placement. Slide the stem ends into the last beads to form a circle. If the stem is

not completely covered by the beads, use wire cutters to cut the ends off. **To clasp:** Fold the lacing through the beaded circle to make a loop. Bring the knotted end through the loop and tighten.

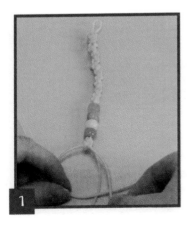

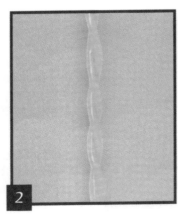

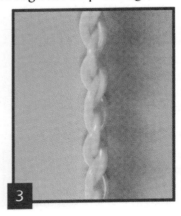

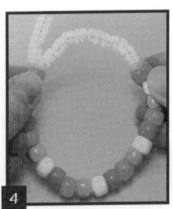

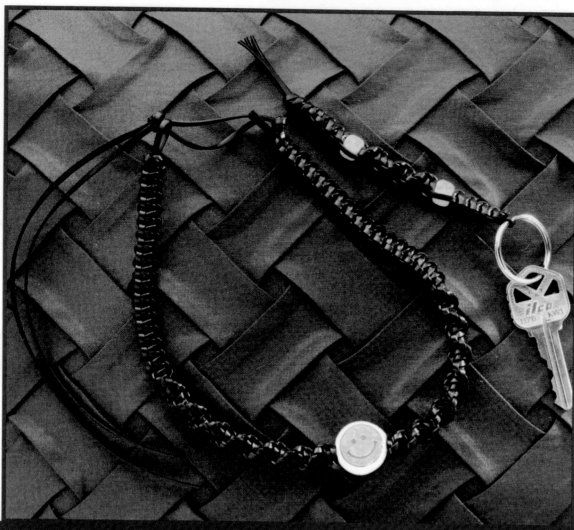

8½ yards of matte black flat plastic lacing
¾" wide yellow smiley face ceramic bead with a lengthwise hole
two ¼" wide yellow plastic pony beads
1" wide silver split ring
basic supplies (see page 1)

SMILEY FACE CHOKER & KEY RING SET

1 Choker: Cut a 1-yard and a 5-yard black lacing length. Fold the 1-yard length in half. Tie the 5-yard length in a square knot (see page 11) just below the fold to form a ½" loop.

2 Square knot braid for 3", then half knot braid (see page 14) with the two strands in the center for 3". Slide the smiley face bead over the center two strands, then half knot braid for 3". Square knot braid for 3", then tie the ends in an overhand knot (see page 18).
To clasp: Tie the loose ends through the beginning loop. Trim the ends or leave them long as shown.

3 Key ring: Cut an 18" and a 2-yard black lacing length. Fold the 18" length in half through the ring. Tie the 2-yard length in a square knot around the 18" length just below the key ring. Square knot braid for ¾", then place a bead on the center strands. Half knot braid for 1" then slide the remaining bead on the center strands. Square knot braid for 1" and tie the ends in an overhand knot. Trim the ends to 1".

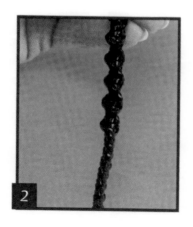

HOW TO SPIRAL BRAID
3–4 lengths of plastic lacing as specified for the project, one 3 times longer than the others

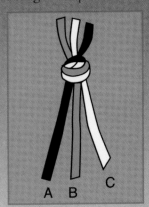 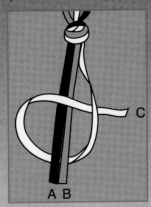  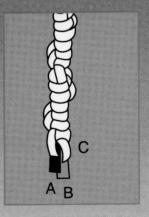

1 Knot all the strands together. Label the short strands A and B, the long strand C. (Strands A and B are the core strands and will not be worked—if you started with four strands, you will have three core strands instead of two.)

2 Bring strand C behind A and B, then over A and B and through the loop made by C.

3 Pull C tightly around A and B.

4 Repeat steps 2–3 until you have reached the length you want. Tie ends in an overhand knot.

PURPLE SPIRAL SET

4 yards of purple round plastic lacing
3/4" wide white heart bead with a lengthwise hole
two 1/2" wide white heart pony beads
seven 1/4" wide bright pink pony beads
2 gold earwires
basic supplies (see page 1)

1 **Bracelet:** Cut a 1-yard and a 2-yard purple lacing length. Fold the 1-yard length in half and place the 2-yard end in the fold. Tie both pieces in an overhand knot (see page 18) 1/2" from the fold to form a loop. Trim the ends to 1/2".

2 Spiral braid (see spiral braid instructions above) for 3", then slide a pink bead, heart bead and pink bead over all the strands. Spiral braid for 3".

3 Tie the ends in an overhand knot. Place a pink bead over one strand, tie two strands in an overhand knot and trim the remaining strand to 1/4". **To clasp:** place the end bead through the beginning loop.

4 **Each earring:** Cut an 18" purple lacing length. Fold it in half through the bottom of the earwire. Tie an overhand knot, then place a pink bead, heart bead and pink bead over both strands. Tie another overhand knot. Trim the ends to 3/4". Repeat for the other earring.

16

for each:
basic supplies (see page 1)

wreath:
4½ yards of green flat plastic lacing
12" of ⅜" wide red satin ribbon
½ wide gold jingle bell

candy cane:
flat plastic lacing: 1⅓ yards of white, 1⅓ yards of red
red chenille stem
12" length of ⅜" wide green satin ribbon

SPIRAL WREATH & CANDY CANE

1 **Wreath:** Hold your fingers together and wrap the green lacing around them ten times to make a ring about 2" wide. Wrap a piece of tape around the ring to hold the strands together, leaving the loose end free. Holding the ring together with one hand and use the other to wrap the loose end in a spiral braid (see page 16) around the ring.

2 When you have braided all the way around the ring, fold the end to make a loop and tie it in an overhand knot (see page 18) close to wreath. Place the bell on the center of the ribbon. Tie the red ribbon in a shoestring bow with ½" loops and 2" tails.

Glue it to the wreath front as shown in the large photo. Trim the ribbon ends diagonally.

3 **Candy cane:** Cut the red chenille stem to 9". Glue the lacing ¼" from the stem end and fold the stem end over the lacing as shown. Half knot braid with the chenille stem in the center until you are ¼" from the end of the stem. Knot and glue the strands together.

4 Bend the braid into a candy cane shape. Tie the green ribbon in a shoestring bow with ½" loops and 2" tails. Glue it to the candy cane as shown in the large photo. Trim the ribbon ends diagonally.

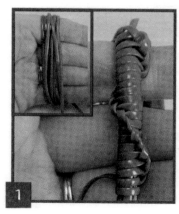

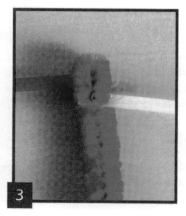
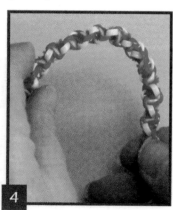